Parrots

Bernard Stonehouse

Animals of the World

ISBN 0 85340 802 5
© Copyright 1981 Wayland Publishers Limited

First published in 1981 by
Wayland Publishers Limited
49 Lansdowne Place, Hove
East Sussex BN3 1HF, England

Typesetting in the U.K. by Direct Image Photosetting, Hove.
Printed in Italy by G. Canale & C.S.p.A., Turin
Bound in the U.K. by The Pitman Press, Bath

About this book

Parrots are often kept as pets, but do you know how they live in the wild? This book describes a very different way of life to that of cage birds. It tells you how parrots feed, court, nest and breed. How do parrots learn to talk? Why are they so brightly coloured? In this delightful book Bernard Stonehouse gives insights into the lives of these unusual birds.

About the author

Dr Bernard Stonehouse is the author of many publications on ethology and ecology, and is Editor of the series *Biology and Environment*. He is Chairman of the Postgraduate School of Studies in Environmental Science at the University of Bradford. His main interest is in environmental and natural history education.

Contents

1 The parrots

The parrots are a family of lively, noisy birds with big nutcracker bills, and beautiful, often brightly-coloured plumage. They live mainly in tropical countries, but are common in temperate climates too. Everyone likes parrots: they are popular in zoos, where they are easy to keep, and have long been kept as household pets. Large pet shops usually have one or two big parrots for sale — often colourful macaws or African greys — and perhaps a cage of smaller parrakeets, rosellas or love-birds. Nearly every pet shop sells green, yellow or blue budgerigars, the most popular cage birds of all. In fact they are small parrots that live in their thousands in the dry forests and grasslands of Australia.

However well they are cared for in captivity, parrots are naturally more at home in the wild, where they can spread their wings and show their brilliant feathers. Occasionally flocks of wild parrots can be seen in Europe, among less exotic birds such as blackbirds,

A Pale-headed rosella, one of the small long-tailed parrots of north-eastern Australia

9

A Yellow-fronted Amazon parrot. Always inquisitive and busy, parrots like to play with twigs and leaves

starlings and rooks. These parrots are always descend-ants of birds that have escaped from captivity and survived to breed on their own. There may even be enough of them to become a nuisance to farmers and fruitgrowers, because they eat buds, seeds and fruit, and can do a lot of damage with their strong bills.

Parrots live mostly in hot climates, usually in forests or on savanna grasslands where there are plenty of

10

A South American Green-winged macaw. The red stripes on the face are rows of tiny feathers

trees. Many species live in Central and South America, and dozens of different kinds of parrot inhabit the forests of Africa and tropical Asia. Australia, New Guinea and the Pacific Islands, too, have parrots, including some of the smallest and most colourful varieties. Not all parrots are tropical; they live in temperate countries too. Several species of parrot are to be found in New Zealand, some living high in the

11

Perhaps the best known of all parrots is the budgerigar, a small seed-eating bird of the Australian desert

mountains, where they often have to dig in the snow for food. Parrots even live in the cold, windswept forests at the southern tip of South America, and on subantarctic islands south of New Zealand and Australia, where they nest close to penguins and albatrosses.

There are no native wild parrots living in Europe today — only escaped birds and their descendants.

A male King parakeet; these small birds live in Australian coastal and mountain forests

Until quite recently there was a species found only in North America. These native Carolina parrots lived in the southern forests. They were kept as pets by Indians, and when the settlers came to America, they also tamed the parrots. But the birds were hunted too much, their forest was cut down to clear the land, and the last few native Carolina parrots disappeared early in the present century.

14

During the past few hundred thousand years, as Man has continued to colonize uninhabited areas of the earth, parrots have been hunted more and more. In places where they are plentiful they are usually easy to catch. Naturally inquisitive, they walk readily into traps, and can be caught with boomerangs or arrows. Hungry people find them good to eat, and their feathers have always been in demand for decoration, even in modern times. It is not surprising that many kinds of parrot have become extinct during the past few hundred years, and that several species today are rare — reduced in numbers to just a few individuals.

At present there are about 320 different kinds of parrot alive in the world. Because of their popularity, many attempts have been made to group them in different ways to show how they are related to each other. Most biologists today divide the family of parrots into eight subfamilies, which are dealt with in later chapters of this book. But first, let us look at parrots themselves, and see what kind of birds they really are.

A Blue-headed parrot; this species lives in the tropical forests of South America

2 What is a parrot?

What is a parrot? How can you tell one from other birds? A good way to distinguish any bird from another is to look first at its bill and feet. Both are specially shaped for the particular kind of life that the bird leads, and parrots show this very clearly.

Every parrot has a strong, hooked bill that looks as though it is shaped to crack nuts and seeds. The upper part is usually long, with ridges inside and a blunt, down-curving point. The lower part, smaller and tucked underneath, may be pointed or deeply grooved. Both are covered with a thick horny sheath that grows in layers throughout the bird's life, and flakes away to give edges that always stay sharp. Between them the two halves of the bill form tough, strong cutters and crushers.

The best way to see how a bill works is to watch a parrot eating a nut or big seed. It is grasped by the bill and the thick muscular tongue turns and shifts it to

This Blue-and-gold macaw holds a nut firmly in its flexible toes, whilst stripping off the shell with its tongue and bill

17

The red headband of this Military macaw hides the cere and nostrils, and covers the movable hinge that helps a parrot's bill to grip tightly

find the weakest part. Then the muscles tighten, and the sharp edges crush and splinter the shell. It is as well to keep your fingers away; even a playful bite from a parrot can be painful and cut very deeply. Not all parrots eat nuts and seeds, but their ancestors probably did in the past, and the modern ones have kept the same basic shape of bill because it is useful for other kinds of food too. Parrots always have a patch of

18

Notice the soft cere surrounding the parrot's nostrils

soft skin at the top of the bill, called the cere, surrounding the nostrils. In some it is hidden by feathers, but others show it clearly. Male budgerigars have a blue cere, females have a pale blue or brown one.

The feet are different from those of nearly all other birds. Look carefully at a parrot or budgerigar on a perch, then at a sparrow, gull or blackbird, and you

Above *The hard casing of the Yellow-fronted Amazon parrot's bill grows throughout life, flaking away so that the edges are razor-sharp*

Right *Blue-and-gold macaws show the typical parrot features—strong bills and feet with two toes pointing forward*

will see the difference straight away. Most birds' feet have three toes pointing forward, and one much smaller toe pointing backward, to help them balance when walking. However parrots have two toes pointing forward and two pointing backward. This is a much better arrangement for birds that spend most

20

22

of their lives climbing and swinging on branches, because it gives them a particularly firm wrap-around grip. In fact they can turn their outer toe either forward or backward, which is very useful when they want to hold a slippery round nut or fruit. The claws are always long and sharp, helping them to cling tightly when climbing. Parrots use both bill and claws to fight and can defend themselves well.

Parrots are distinctively coloured — few other kinds of bird have such brilliantly patterned or shiny plumage as most of the parrots. Many are vivid red, yellow, green, purple or blue. The macaws are by far the brightest, with a variety of different hues. Even the black, brown or grey parrot somehow manages to look colourful. It often has a flash of red or white under the wings or among the tail feathers, and shiny, iridescent patches that flash green or blue in the sun.

Colours are important in courtship, threat displays, and also just to keep track of each other. Parrots are very sociable birds, and like to be with others of their kind. Their brightly-coloured feathers help them to spot each other and keep together both in the dim light of the forest and the dazzling sunshine of the open plains.

Just as important for preventing any member of the

A Pale-headed rosella of north-eastern Australia, stripping seeds from a branch group from straying, are their whistles and harsh, cackling calls, which they make constantly as they move through the trees. Pairs and family groups chatter as they huddle together on branches. It sounds as though they always have a lot to say to each other, but this is probably just to make sure that they all stay within the safety of the group. One parrot on its own would be very easy prey for hawks and other predators; a hundred or a thousand together are much safer. When they are in pairs and small groups they show each other a lot of attention and affection — you can see that even caged parrots are usually more lively and active when there are several of them together.

One of the reasons that has helped to make parrots popular is their strange ability to talk, and to make noises like doors banging, kettles whistling and even dogs barking. Their real talent is imitation. In the forest they would normally be hearing and imitating the sounds made by their parents and the other birds in their flock, so that each flock of birds can identify its own members. Captive parrots hear only human voices and household noises, so they repeat the sounds that they hear frequently, sometimes with surprising accuracy. Do they understand what they are saying? Not really — you cannot hold a conversation with a parrot for long. But they often make the appropriate remark — like 'hello' when you come in and 'goodbye' when you go out, because they associate the words

*An Australian King parakeet. Parrots' brilliant colours help
them to recognize each other even in dark forests*

with the actions. There is a parrot in Edinburgh Zoo,
very popular with school parties, that always makes
sympathetic crying noises when it hears a child crying
nearby. That makes the child laugh, so the parrot
laughs too.

Parrots have broad rounded wings that lift them
quickly off the ground and give them a good turn of
speed — rather like pheasants or partridges. The tail is
broad, and often kite-shaped, to give them extra lift.
They seldom fly fast for very long, though they can

25

A Fischer's lovebird in flight: when they are flying you can see the beautiful colours in a parrot's plumage

cover long distances when searching for food and water during droughts. In the forest they flutter and crash from branch to branch, walking and climbing as much as flying. In open country they swoop and glide from tree to tree, landing with a rush of wings and a chatter of excitement. Some of the heavy ground-living parrots have lost most of their powers of flight; they climb trees and rocks, then just use their wings to glide down again. Others never fly at all. Parrots that have spent many years in cages or chained to perches,

26

may have forgotten how to fly, or lost their self-confidence. They soon learn again when given the chance. Once you have seen a big parrot in flight, you may never want to see one chained up or kept in a small cage again.

3 Family life

Whether they live in large or small flocks, parrots of all kinds pair off for breeding. Each pair finds a nest site — often a hole in a log or hollow tree, or even in a drain-pipe — and defends it against neighbours that may try to take it over. If the hole is too small, they use their strong bill to enlarge it, making it just big enough to get through, but no more. Then one of them (usually the female) can sit inside and defend it while the other forages for food.

Where there are dozens of pairs of flocking parrots, all of them ready to nest at once, competition for suitable nesting space may be keen, with a lot of jostling and fighting for sites. Eventually they settle down to a compromise, and in the end there may be six or eight pairs nesting together as very close neighbours, in a single hollow log, each site a few centimetres from the next.

Parrots make only a small nest, often just a shallow

Wild budgerigars nest in hollow trees and logs, often in groups of several hundred pairs

Parrots make their nest-hole just big enough to get through

bowl scraped in the ground, with a few scraps of rotten wood or well-chewed sticks in the bottom. A few line their nest hole with grass or leaves. One species, the Quaker parakeet of South America, has the unusual habit of building huge communal nests of twigs and grass, with cavities for several pairs. In many species, (budgerigars for example) the hen occupies the nest for several days before the eggs are laid, while the cock

These Rose-ringed parakeets are inspecting a possible nest site

forages for food. He collects seeds and insects and carries them to her in his crop. This saves the hen from having to hunt for her own food, so that all her energy can go into producing the clutch of eggs. The darkness of the nest cavity, and the male's chattering and warbling outside, stimulate her ovaries into production. The eggs are white and almost round with a rough, chalky surface, and are laid over a period of a few days. Lories and lorikeets lay only two eggs, but most parrots produce three to six, and some of the small ones lay as many as eight or nine.

Incubation takes three to four weeks. Nesting in hollows and secluded corners ensures that the eggs are hidden from many kinds of predator. Snakes, lizards, rats and a host of other hunters are always on the look-out for food, and the pair may have to defend their

Macaw chicks have no feathers when they are born but they will eventually grow a beautiful blue and yellow plumage

nest, or escape hurriedly, several times during incubation. In some species only the hen incubates, in others the two parents take turns. The young hatch out over several days. Naked and helpless, they need to be kept constantly warm for the first few days of life, so the incubating parent sits close. By the time the last chick has hatched, the first is starting to grow a soft, protective down, and has already managed to sit up.

Baby budgerigars in a nest box. The eldest has begun to grow downy feathers, while the youngest are still unhatched

From the start the first chicks are always stronger and better able to compete for the food that the parents bring back to them. In a good season all the chicks will probably be reared, but in a bad one, when food is scarce, only the first one or two of the clutch will survive.

With good feeding by hard-working parents, the chicks will be ready to leave the nest in three or four weeks (longer in some of the bigger species) and begin to fly when their wing and tail feathers are properly grown. The parents continue to feed them for some weeks while the chicks fly along with the rest of the flock. During this time the chicks learn to forage for themselves, feeding where the others feed, discovering which seeds and twigs are good to eat, and which flowers carry the nectar. Many young birds breed when they are one year old; in some of the larger parrots maturity is delayed for two or three seasons.

Parrots are usually seasonal breeders, though in the tropics the difference between summer and winter may be slight. Spring and summer are the normal times for breeding, because this is when food starts to be plentiful, and well-fed chicks have a better chance of surviving than hungry ones. In some parts of the world, like the Australian desert, the parrots breed

A South American Quaker parakeet; this species builds large nests in which several families live together

35

A small flock of wild budgerigars, swarming to drink at an Australian desert waterhole

only during the rainy seasons. Budgerigar flocks may drift for months over the dry plains until they find a place where recent heavy rainfall has caused the grass to grow. Then they settle and start to breed quickly, and their chicks are born just as the grass is producing its seed-heads. A long drought means that there is little

or no breeding, and it causes many millions of birds to
die of overheating and exhaustion. There are stories
told of huge flocks of parrots descending on water-
holes in the desert, and of thousands of the birds
drowning because they all scramble to the water to
drink at once.

4 Popular parrots

Most of the world's parrots live in the great southern continents. The greatest variety of species, and quite possibly the greatest number of individuals, are found in Australasia (Australia, New Zealand, New Guinea and the nearby islands). All of the eight subfamilies of parrots can be found there, and four of these are not found outside Australasia. Many of the popular species that are kept as pets and in zoos originally came from Australia itself. Not only are they lively and colourful birds, but they are also among the most hardy of parrots. They need to be tough to survive drought and food shortages in the deserts of the Australian outback, and so these strong species live longest in captivity.

Budgerigars are a good example of seed-eating birds that survive well under the harsh conditions of the Australian desert. Wild budgerigars are green, or occasionally yellow, in their native Australia; the blue,

A Fischer's lovebird; this colourful East African parrot thrives in aviaries

mauve and other varieties familiar as cage birds have all been developed by breeders. They belong to the great subfamily of parrots called parakeets — small parrots with long tails found throughout the tropics.

Crimson and Eastern rosellas, also popular as cage birds, are forest parakeets of Australia. South American parakeets, called conures, are mostly green, with a fully-feathered face and a large, bulbous bill. South African parakeets include the popular love-

A friendly pair of Masked lovebirds. Like all parrots, lovebirds are very sociable and like to have others of their kind around

This bright Crimson rosella is easy to see even at dusk

birds, small and brilliantly coloured, often with a green body and orange, red or yellow upper feathers. Immensely sociable, the lovebirds like to sit closely in pairs, billing, preening and chattering to each other. Several species of lovebird build nests of grass and leaves, which they tear into convenient lengths and carry among their feathers to the nest site. Asian members of the group include the curious little Bat or Hanging parakeets, that sleep hanging upside

41

42

Above A Blue-streaked lory, a parrot of the Indonesian forest

Left A Blue-crowned Hanging parrot. These tiny birds sleep hanging upside down from branches

down from their roost like bats. Only 12 to 15 cm long (5 to 6 in), they are small enough to climb among flowers and take nectar. They also like to eat fruit and seeds, and probably feed their young on insects.

Lories and lorikeets are a separate subfamily of parrots that are particularly fond of nectar. They are similar except for their colouring. Lories are usually red, with splashes of yellow and green on them, while lorikeets are mostly green with brilliant patches of yellow, red or blue. There are about 25 species of lory

Above *A Dusky lory, a forest parrot of New Guinea and Papua that feeds on nectar from flowers*

Right *Military macaws. When they are flying their broad tail spreads into a green triangle with blue and red stripes*

and 30 species of lorikeet living in the forests of the East Indies, Australasia and islands of the South Pacific Ocean.

Lorikeets tend to be slightly smaller than lories, with a longer and more slender tail. Both fly in nomadic flocks, often of several hundred. When they settle on trees in chattering swarms, they look like clusters of flowers. Flowering trees are in fact their main interest, for they feed mostly on nectar and pollen, which they find by tearing the blossoms apart. They have a sharp bill for opening the flowers, and a tongue with a brush-like tip for licking out the nectar and pollen. Fruit, buds, and possibly insects are also

included in their diet.

African Grey parrots are widespread in the forests of Africa south of the Sahara; and a race with dark slate-grey plumage lives on islands in the Gulf of Guinea. Perhaps the best mimics and talkers of all, they have long been popular house pets. Many stories are told of the intelligence and liveliness of these birds, and of their longevity — they may live for thirty or forty years in captivity, and possibly longer. In the wild they are the shy birds of the forest and we know very little about

African Grey parrots may live to be as old as thirty or forty years

These two macaws—the Red-and-blue, and the Military, get on well together and may even mate in captivity

how they live. Once well established in aviaries they breed quite freely, producing clutches of four eggs. The hen usually does most of the incubating, but both parents take an interest in the chicks, feeding and clucking over them.

The largest and brightest of the parrots seen in captivity are the macaws. These are a group of Central and South American parrots, often about a metre long (over 3ft) from huge hooked bill to tail. They are among the most colourful of all birds, with brilliant

47

48

feathers of scarlet, gold, blue and green. The face is often naked or only lightly feathered (as in many big parrots) and the bill may be pink or black. There are about eighteen natural species, but hybrid forms have been produced by cross-breeding in aviaries. There may well have been more species before Man began to hunt macaws for their beautiful feathers, and some small island bird populations — perhaps even large mainland populations as well — have been hunted to extinction.

Many macaws and other parrots are captured each year, to be transported about the world and sold as cage birds. This is sometimes a cruel business, with thousands of birds dying in overcrowded cages in the cargo holds of ships and aircraft. Fortunately this trade is decreasing, because more and more countries are protecting their birds instead of allowing them to be sold, and because transportation costs are rising. So more attention is being paid to rearing birds in captivity, and the wild stocks are less endangered. However, there are still problems, because huge areas of tropical forests are cut down each year, and with them go the homes of many of the world's most beautiful and colourful parrots.

A Sulphur-crested cockatoo. The cockatoo's crest normally lies flat, but is raised when the bird is alarmed or angry

5 Strange and rare parrots

There are dozens of different kinds of parrot that have never or very seldom been kept in captivity, some because they live in out-of-the-way corners of the world, others because they are difficult to keep in cages and aviaries. There are many species that are now extremely rare, usually through over-hunting or because their habitat (the forest or grasslands in which they live) is being destroyed.

One group of parrots that has proved almost impossible to keep for long in captivity is the Pygmy parrot, the smallest parrot of all, that lives in the forests of New Guinea and some of its neighbouring islands. These tiny birds measuring only 8 to 10 cm long (3 to 4 in) are mostly bright green with brilliant flashes of contrasting colour on the head and body. They dig their nesting burrows in the nests of termites (ant-like insects that build mounds of mud on the ground or in trees). Pygmy parrots feed on insects,

This Pesquet's parrot is a rare fruit-eating species living in the mountains of New Guinea

The Kakapo or Owl-parrot's drab colours blend into the forest vegetation of New Zealand where it lives

seeds and lichens, and find a lot of their food by digging in the cracks and crevices of tree bark, running up and down the trunks like tiny woodpeckers. Their claws are especially long and sharp, to help them hold on, and their tail feathers are stiff to help them balance.

One of the strangest and rarest of parrots is the Kakapo or Owl parrot of New Zealand. It lives in the rainforests among the fiords and mountains of New Zealand's South Island and neighbouring Stewart

Island. Once it was more widespread, but Man himself and the animals he brought with him — dogs, cats and weasels especially — exterminated the parrots in all but the remotest corners. Dull yellowy-green and brown, with the owl-like face which gives it its name, and soft plumage, the Kakapo is nocturnal and almost flightless. Much of its time is spent on the ground, where it eats grass, ferns, mosses and lichens, but Kakapos also climb trees and glide down again. They are reported to hunt lizards, and many also eat flowers for their pollen and nectar. Though it is almost

The Kakariki or Yellow-fronted parakeet, is a small bird of the forests and mountains of southern New Zealand

Above *A Kea; the name of this parrot of the New Zealand forests and mountains comes from its call*

Left *When these colourful Blue-rumped parrots of Malaya are flying you can see brilliant red flashes under their wings*

impossible to estimate their numbers in the depths of the dripping rainforests, there may well be only a few hundred of this unique species left.

Almost as strange, though far more numerous, is the Kea, another yellowy-green parrot of New Zealand. Keas are a more uniformly dull green, with bright crimson patches under the wing that flash when they take off. They are strong fliers, and beat against the wind, soaring over the mountain country of the South Island, which is their only home. They divide their time between the high alpine grasslands and the upland forests, breeding in rock crevices and tunnels, or in hollow logs. Their slender, hooked bill scrapes lichens, buds and bark from trees, and can also be used to scrape grubs and insects from the soil. Keas have also taken to eating the fat and meat from dead sheep. Farmers in the mountain areas have destroyed many hundreds of the birds in the belief that they may attack live sheep, though the case against them is uncertain. Keas are playful and inquisitive, and can be very tame. Campers are often awakened at dawn by Keas bouncing and sliding on their tent roof, and then walking inside to join them at breakfast.

The names of several types of parrot appear today in the *Red Data Book*, which is the list of species now rare and believed to be in danger of extinction. It is always a tragedy when a species of plant or animal is lost through Man's carelessness or greed, and particularly so when species as lively, cheerful and colourful as the parrots disappears. Yet many have been lost in the last two or three centuries, and others will certainly go unless we make special efforts to save them.

This Yellow-fronted Amazon parrot is enjoying a shower of rain

Glossary

AVIARY   A large enclosure in which birds are kept.

CERE   A patch of soft skin at the top of the bill, surrounding the nostrils.

COMMUNAL NEST   A nest where several pairs of birds live together.

COURTSHIP   The means by which a male attracts a female to be his mate.

CROP   The throat pouch used for storing food.

DOWN   The fine powdery feathers that are the first plumage of a baby bird.

DROUGHT   A shortage of rain over a long period of time.

FORAGE   To search for food.

HYBRID   Offspring whose parents are of different breeds or species.

INCUBATION   The process of hatching an egg by keeping it warm.

58

IRIDESCENT   Displaying a spectrum of colours that shimmer and change as the person looking at it changes position.

LICHEN   A fungus-like plant which grows on the surface of rocks and tree trunks.

NECTAR   Sweet liquid produced by flowers.

NOMADIC FLOCKS   Flocks of birds without a fixed home which drift from place to place.

OVARIES   The part of the female body where the egg cells are formed.

PLUMAGE   A covering of feathers.

PREDATOR   A creature that hunts and eats other animals.

SUBFAMILY   A division of a larger group.

TEMPERATE CLIMATE   Moderate climate.

THREAT DISPLAY   A display of aggression by squawking and puffing up feathers to defend territory or mate.

Picture Acknowledgements

Aquila photographics 41; Ardea 30, 31, 33; Bruce Coleman Limited, by the following photographers Jen and Des Bartlett (endpapers), Jane Burton (front cover), 10, 16, 57, Bruce Coleman 8, 22, 36-7, 38, 42, 44, 48, Francisco Erize 25, Fritz Prenzel 25, Hans Reinhard 12, 18, 20, 26, 27, 40, 47, 54, H. Rivarola 35, V. Serventy 28, M. F. Soper 52, 53, 55, Lynn M. Stone (back cover), Rod Williams 43, Joseph P. Wormer 50; Natural History Photographic Agency 46; John Topham Picture Library 11, 32, 45; Zefa R. Halin 19, G. Krolin 21, K. Heinz Zawodsky 14.

60

Index